I0220369

# Words on Birds II

## Feathered Friends of the Dandenongs

Kathie M. Thomas

9780975728529
Author: Kathie M. Thomas
Photography: Kathie M. Thomas
Printer: Ingram Spark

No part of this publication may be reproduced in whole, or in part, or stored in a retrieval system, or transmitted in any form or by any means, electronic, mechanical, photocopying, recording, or otherwise, without written permission of the copyright owner.
For information regarding permission contact:
Kathie M. Thomas, dandenong-ranges-photography.com.au

Copyright © 2021 by Kathie M. Thomas
All rights reserved.

*This second book is dedicated to my friends and family and is about another collection of birds found in the Dandenong Ranges. It is not complete but covers a further 30+ birds seen here in the Dandenongs – did you know there were so many?*

*We are, indeed, very blessed to have them.*

*For:  Oliver, Morgan, Claudia, Katara, Josiah, Michael, Dana and Benaiah who remain my inspiration and joy for sharing the love of nature that surrounds us.*

*Kathie M. Thomas*

**Locations:**
Birds in this book have been seen at the following places: Birdsland Reserve in Belgrave Heights; my garden in Selby; Grants Picnic Grounds and Sherbrooke Forest in Kallista; George Tindale Gardens in Sherbrooke, Dandenong Ranges Botanic Gardens in Olinda, Lillydale Lake, and Lysterfield Lake.

## List of birds in this book:

| | |
|---|---|
| Black-faced Cuckoo-shrike | Little Black Cormorant |
| Chestnut Teal | Magpie-lark |
| Common Blackbird | Masked Lapwing |
| Common Bronzewing | Mistletoe Bird |
| Corella (Little and Long-billed) | Musk Duck |
| Crescent Honeyeater | Nankeen Night-Heron |
| Crested Pigeon | Noisy Miner |
| Crested Shrike Tit | Red-browed Finch |
| Dusky Moorhen | Reed Warbler |
| Eastern Rosella | Rufous Whistler |
| Eastern Yellow Robin | Scarlet Honeyeater |
| Great Egret | Silvereye |
| Grey Currawong | Wedge-tailed Eagle |
| Grey Shrike-thrush | Welcome Swallow |
| Grey Teal Duck | White Ibis |
| Hardhead Duck | White-browed Scrubwren |
| Lewin's Honeyeater | Yellow-faced Honeyeater |

# Black-faced Cuckoo-shrike

This bird is a medium size with black face and grey back, wings and tail. It likes to live in bushland areas but can be found in city suburbs as well.

The Black-faced Cuckoo-shrike feeds on insects as well as things like snails, slugs, worms and similar.

They can sometimes be seen catching insects in the air but mostly from trees and bushes.

You might even see one in your garden!

Black-faced
Cuckoo-shrike

# Chestnut Teal Duck

*The Chestnut Teal Duck is a pretty duck. The male has a dark green head that shines in the sun and a pretty chestnut brown body. The female is more plain, brown and grey colour but with similar markings to the male.*

*They hang around lakes and other wetland areas and feed upon aquatic vegetation, often where the water is shallow, but will upend in deeper water to get a feed. Maybe you've seen an upside-down duck?*

# CHESTNUT TEAL
# DUCK

# Common Blackbird

This bird is not native to Australia but was introduced in Melbourne in the 1850s. They are a beautiful songbird and I'm sure you would have heard one singing near where you live.

When full grown the males are black with a bright orange beak but the females are a dull brown. The juveniles are a brighter brown colour.

They eat insects, worms, snails, spiders and also seeds and fruits.

Have you seen one of these birds? Maybe in your garden. The male is black and the female brown

# COMMON BLACKBIRD

# Common Bronzewing

*These are very common birds in our area. They are a medium sized but heavily built pigeon with beautiful colouring and markings on their wings. The male has a yellow-white forehead and pink breast.*

*You can find them in bushland, or urban areas.*

*They like to feed on seeds and vegetable matter and are often found in pairs, or sometimes alone. Usually not very far from water.*

*They make a deep ooom, oom sound over and over again.*

A pretty bird

# COMMON BRONZEWING

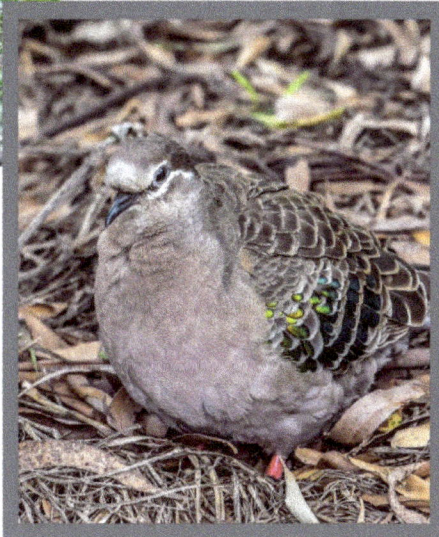

# Corella

There are two types of Corella. The Little Corella with a short beak, and the Long-billed Corella with a long curved beak. Both birds are similar in plumage, with white bodies, and the blue surround around the eyes and the pale rose-pink patch between the eye and bill. The long-billed has an orange band on the throat.

These birds usually hang around in noisy flocks, sometimes with cockatoos and galahs, and feed mainly on the ground on grains and seeds.

**CORELLAS**

# Crescent Honeyeater

*I was so excited when I saw this little bird. I'd not seen one before and they're probably not as common as other small honeyeaters. They migrate to lower elevations during Autumn.*

*They have a long-curved bill (similar to the spinebill) and have an interesting dark crescent across each side of the breast, outlined below with a white line. Females are smaller and are olive brown in colour. They feed on nectar, fruit and insects.*

*They can sometimes be mistaken for New Holland Honeyeaters (See Book 1).*

A small bird

**CRESCENT HONEYEATER**

## Crested Pigeon

Once a common arid living bird they gradually moved closer to the coast, starting in Adelaide, and later Brisbane and Perth. They're now seen in the other state capitals and suburbs too. You may have seen them near your home.

I love the beautiful colours on their wings. They make a whistling sound when flying. They are one of only two pigeons that have an erect crest. They eat seeds, leaves and insects.

# Crested Pigeon

# Crested Shrike-tit

*This is a small-medium sized bird and has an amazing black and white striped head and neck with a small crest that will often flatten on the crown (top).*

*I was so excited to see one of these in my own garden but only the once, so far. They usually inhabit open forests and woodland. Maybe you've seen one too?*

*These birds are insect eaters but also like fruit and seeds.*

Has a small crest

# CRESTED
# SHRIKE-TIT

# Dusky Moorhen

Around the same size as the Eurasian Coot (See Book 1) and belongs to the rail family. They hang around lakes, creeks and other water areas. Where the Coot has a white beak, the Moorhen has a red-orange bill with a yellow tip.

The Dusky Moorhen feeds in the water but also on land, foraging for algae, water plants and grasses, and seeds and fruits as well as invertebrates (insects and water life).

A water bird

# DUSKY MOORHEN

# Eastern Rosella

A medium sized bird, same as the Crimson Rosella (See Book 1); these birds have a pretty mix of colours: red, yellow, green, blue and white.

They can often be seen feeding on the ground amongst grasses, enjoying the seeds, fruits, buds, nectar, insects and flowers but will fly up into trees if disturbed, hiding amongst the foliage.

Their patterned plumage makes it easy for them to hide in trees and be undetected by potential predators.

# Eastern Rosella

# Eastern Yellow Robin

*This is one of my favourite little birds. I see them often in the warmer seasons at my home in Selby but you can see them in bushland and forests. They often perch on the side of tree trunks. They have a variety of calls.*

*This robin is known for following people around in the woods, feeding off insects, spiders and other small invertebrate animals disturbed by humans walking around, or other birds scratching.*

# EASTERN YELLOW
# ROBIN

# Fan-tailed Cuckoo

This medium sized bird isn't always around but so worth seeing. It has a trilled call and I had been wondering for some time what the call was till I finally saw the bird. I hear them mostly in Spring and early Summer.

They like to feed on hairy caterpillars but also other insects and larvae. Food is usually found in trees or in flight although they will get food off the ground and then return to perch in a tree to eat.

Fan-tailed Cuckoo

## Grey Currawong

*Very similar to the Pied Currawong (See Book 1), only grey in colour. It has a very different call as well. They like to hang around in forests and woodlands and you can hear their call echoing through the valleys.*

*They eat small animals such as other birds, rodents, frogs, as well as eggs, insects, seeds and fruits. We often hear and see them late summer through autumn once our fig tree is in fruit.*

One of three
Currawong species

**GREY
CURRAWONG**

# Grey Shrike-thrush

*This is a beautiful songbird and I love hearing it on our property and in woodlands nearby. While it is considered to be drab in colour, that is grey with some brown, its song more than makes up for that.*

*This bird mostly forages on the ground for food, around fallen branches and on limbs of trees, looking for insects, small mammals, frogs and lizards and even the eggs of other birds.*

# GREY
# SHRIKE-THRUSH

# Grey Teal Duck

*These birds are known as dabbling ducks found in open wetlands throughout Australia. Similar pattern to the Chestnut Teal but a lighter, grey-brown colour.*

*I sometimes see them at Birdsland Reserve, usually during nesting season in spring. They are known to travel great distances in search of water and will even fly to waterholes in the desert.*

Found in wetlands

GREY TEAL DUCK

# Hardhead Duck

*This duck has an unusual name and used to be known as the white-eyed duck. But the females don't have white eyes at all. Apparently, the name 'hardhead' came from early taxidermists who found the head hard to process.*

*The Hardhead duck is a medium-sized duck which is mainly chocolate brown in colour. It has a white breast patch which is obvious in flight.*

*They eat aquatic plants and animals, particularly mussels and freshwater shellfish.*

# HARDHEAD DUCK

# Lewin's Honeyeater

*The Lewin's Honeyeater loves fruit and can eat off trees, the ground, or even compost heaps. But it will also eat insects and nectar too.*

*It is a small to medium sized bird and is dark green/grey in colour with cream yellow crescent shaped patches by its ears. While mostly seen in northern Queensland it does venture down to Victoria and this particular one was seen in the George Tindale Gardens, Kallista Spring 2020.*

Lewin's
Honeyeater

# Little Black Cormorant

*The Little Black Cormorant usually stays in groups or flocks, rather than individually. I've seen them at Birdsland Reserve at different times. They have a beautiful greenish sheen and a slender grey hooked bill. They also have striking turquoise-blue eyes.*

*They are found mainly in wetland areas but sometimes coastal waters too. They feed on crustaceans and aquatic insects, usually by diving underwater. Their feathers aren't waterproof so they will hold their wings out to dry after fishing.*

Little Black Cormorant

# Magpie-lark

Often goes by different names, including Murray Magpie or Peewee in South Australia, here in Victoria they're called the Magpie-lark.

These birds are seen in parks, gardens and streets but also in bushland and farmland areas. They make nests out of mud and roots.

The Magpie-lark feeds on insects and larvae as well as worms and freshwater invertebrates. Perhaps you've seen one in your garden?

# MAGPIE-LARK

# Masked Lapwing

*These are large ground dwelling birds that are often found in urban areas, setting up nests close to roads, schools and playgrounds, as well as car parks. They have a yellow spur with a black tip and while they appear threatening, don't usually strike what or who they're threatening if you happen to venture on their spot during nesting season.*

*While they nest near where we live, they are wary of people. Their chicks are very cute and fluffy.*
*They feed on insects, larvae and worms. Usually seen in pairs.*

Found in urban
areas

## MASKED LAPWING

# Mistletoe bird

*I've only seen this bird once, while walking at Birdsland but I've heard others have seen them in the hills here too.*

*This small bird flits amongst tree tops and belongs to the flowerpecker family. It's the male that has the bright red throat and chest and the female is grey above, with a white streak below. They are usually seen where mistletoe grows in trees, and they eat the berries which they then pass quickly, allowing mistletoe to grow in other places. This way it has a constant source of food. It also eats insects.*

**MISTLETOE BIRD**

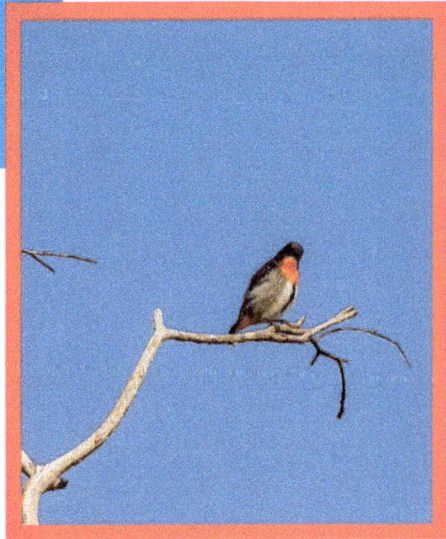

# Musk Duck

*This is a really strange looking bird. I couldn't believe it when I first saw one. The male duck has a large leathery lobe of skin which hangs under its bill and it has a tail that is long and stiff and fans out. He uses this tail to do mating displays when trying to attract a female duck. He also splashes the water while displaying to the female.*

*The female is a smaller bird with just a small lobe.*

*They feed mostly from aquatic animals, insects, crustaceans, snails, shellfish, frogs and ducklings but sometimes seeds of aquatic plants too.*

Musk Duck

# Nankeen Night-Heron

These birds tend to only emerge in the twilight so are often undetected in various areas. I first became aware of this bird when my neighbour said she'd seen a strange bird in a tree over her frog pond. The striped looking bird in the picture opposite is a juvenile Night-Heron.

They usually hang around water regions and feed at night in shallow water on a variety of insects, crustaceans, fish and amphibians, such as frogs.

They make a croaking call.

# NANKEEN
# NIGHT-HERON

## Noisy Miner

*This is a native Australian bird but often mistaken for the Indian Mynah which is brown but has similar facial markings.*

*They are a noisy bird, hence the name, and often repeats its call over and over and over again.*

*Usually found in woodlands and open forests but also common in suburban areas. They feed on nectar, fruits and insects. They can produce more than one brood each season. Both male and female care for the young.*

NOISY MINER

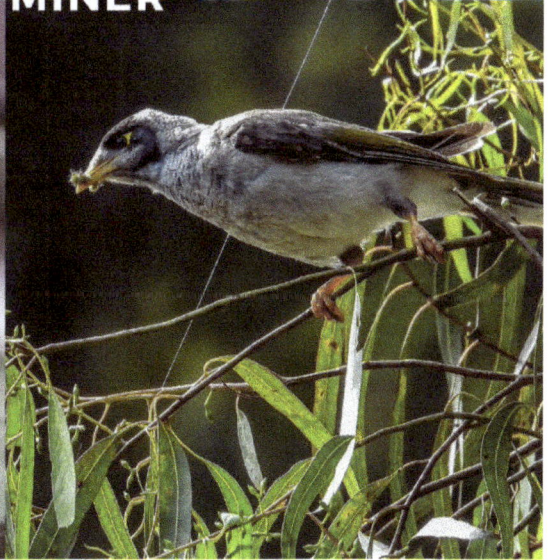

# Red-browed Finch

This bird is a tiny one and is easily recognised by its bright red eyebrow, rump and beak, but is otherwise green and grey on its body.

These birds are usually seen in flocks feeding on grasses and will fly quickly into undergrowth or into trees if disturbed by someone passing by. They are also known as Red-browed Firetails.

These birds feed on seeds and insects on the ground but sometimes will perch on seeding grass heads to feed.

Also known as a
**Red-browed Firetail**

**RED-BROWED FINCH**

# *Reed Warbler*

*This bird arrives in the south eastern parts of our country in spring and then heads north and north-west late summer and early autumn. There is no mistaking when this bird is around as it has a very loud call for a small bird.*

*It lives among reeds but sometimes you get to see it sitting at the top of the reeds as it makes its call. They live mostly near wetlands. They feed off invertebrates, mostly insects that are among the foliage.*

Reed Warbler

# Rufous Whistler

Similar to the Golden Whistler (See Book 1) and has a beautiful song. Sometimes triggered by a loud noise, like a thunderclap or a car passing by. The bird is sometimes referred to as the 'thunder bird' because of this reaction.

As with many birds, the female is less colourful than the male. The Rufous Whistler feeds mainly on insects but sometimes seeds, fruit and leaves. It is rarely seen on the ground, usually high up in trees.

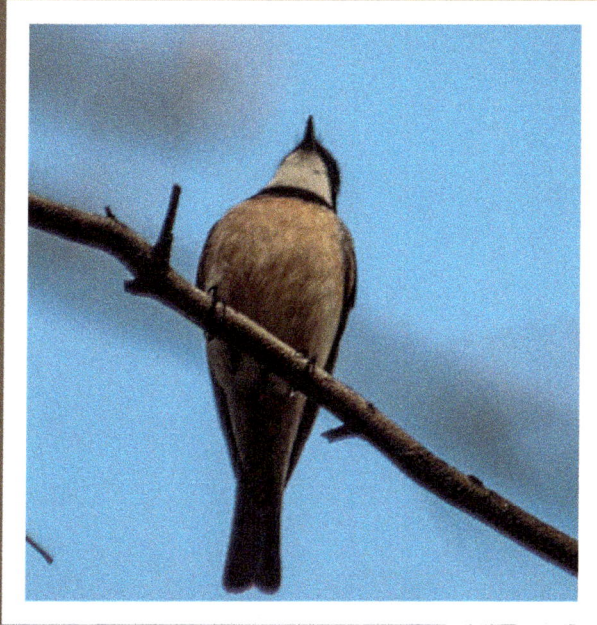

Found in forests and woodlands

RUFOUS WHISTLER

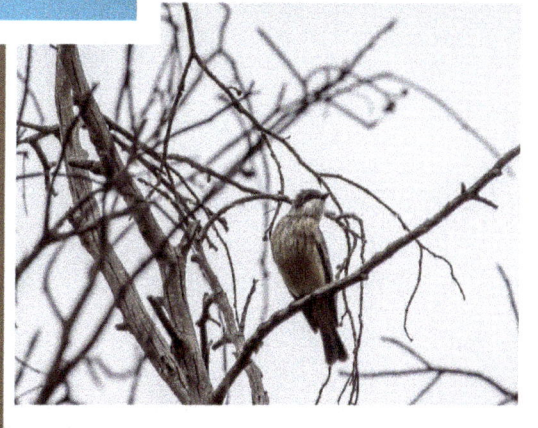

# Scarlet Honeyeater

The adult male Scarlet Honeyeater has very bright red mixed with black on its body and underneath is a light colour. The females and juveniles are a dull brown. They have a short tail.

Often seen alone, or sometimes in pairs, occasionally in flocks high in trees.

Usually found along the east coast of Australia but sometimes further inland in open forests and woodlands. They eat nectar, fruit and insects. I've seen them at Birdsland and in my garden at Selby.

# SCARLET
# HONEYEATER

## Silvereye

*Silvereyes are widespread all over Australia. They are a tiny little bird with a white ring around their eyes. They have an interesting plumage with a grey back and olive-green head and wings, although the ones in the western part of the country are olive green in colour.*

*They eat insects, fruit and nectar and can become pests in commercial orchards. Often seen in groups together.*

SILVEREYE

# Wedge-tailed Eagle

This is the largest bird of prey in Australia with very broad wings, fully feathered legs and a wedge-shaped tail.

They fly high in the sky, making it hard to get a decent photo of one in flight. However, I did get one. Here you can see a magpie telling an eagle off which is common during breeding season. You might see other birds doing this too.

While eagles do feed on rabbits and other small animals, they mostly feed off carrion (dead animals), often found on roads. They also steal chickens if found roaming freely in areas where the eagles live.

Wedge-tailed
Eagle

# Welcome Swallow

*These little birds are seen all over Australia, fluttering, swooping and gliding in search of insects over water and over land. They don't stay still for very long and can be a challenge to photograph.*

*The name 'Welcome' swallow was given to them by sailors who knew that land couldn't be far away whenever they saw these birds. Their nests are made of mud in many places, including under bridges and on walls of buildings.*

# WELCOME
# SWALLOW

# White-browed Scrubwren

These birds are ground dwellers.  Mostly an olive-brown colour, the throat is buff grey.

They feed on insects and other small anthropods (spiders, crustaceans, etc). Occasionally they eat seeds.

Their nest consists of a ball of grasses and other plant material with a tunnel entrance and is usually on the ground, but could be in a tree a few metres up.

# White-browed
# Scrubwren

# White Ibis

*The Australian White Ibis often hang around in flocks and gorge on hordes of insects. In urban areas they can be seen looking through rubbish bins and tips for food. Because their white plumage gets dirty with this activity they are sometimes called 'tip turkeys'.*

*They are almost entirely white with a long black bill and black head and neck.*

*I've seen them in the trees on the island at Birdsland Reserve but I'm sure you may have seen them in many other places too.*

**WHITE IBIS**

# Yellow-Faced Honeyeater

*Like most other honeyeaters in our area, this is an active bird, moving from flower to flower, or tree to tree, seeking out insects, nectar and pollen.*

*They are rarely seen on the ground.*

*You can identify them by their downward curved bill and the yellow face stripe, bordered by black. The rest of the body is a plain brown but with dark grey-brown on the top part of its body.*

*Usually seen in forests and woodlands or near water and wetland areas.*

YELLOW-FACED
HONEYEATER

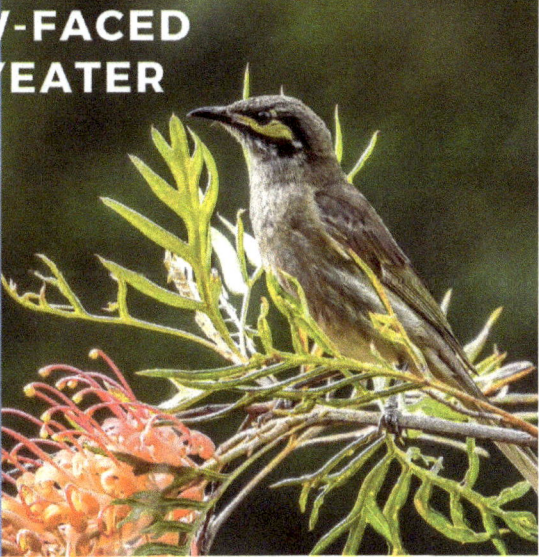

How many of these birds have you seen? Write them down on these pages when you see them so you can keep a record.

| Name of Bird | Date seen | Where seen |
|---|---|---|
| | | |
| | | |
| | | |
| | | |
| | | |
| | | |
| | | |
| | | |
| | | |
| | | |

| Name of Bird | Date seen | Where seen |
|---|---|---|
| | | |
| | | |
| | | |
| | | |
| | | |
| | | |
| | | |
| | | |
| | | |
| | | |
| | | |
| | | |

This is the second book written for children and their families about birds by Kathie.

If you would like to give her feedback, or contact her about anything else, you can find her via her website.

Dandenong Ranges
NATURE PHOTOGRAPHY

www.dandenong-ranges-photography.com.au

www.ingramcontent.com/pod-product-compliance
Lightning Source LLC
Chambersburg PA
CBHW051618030426
42334CB00030B/3237